MADEMOISELLE FIFI

Borgo Press Books by FRANK J. MORLOCK

Castor and Pollux and Other Opera Libretti (Editor)
The Chevalier d'Éon and Other Short Farces (Editor)
Chuzzlewit
Congreve's Comedy of Manners
Crime and Punishment
Cyrano and Molière: Five Plays by or About Molière (Editor)
Doctor Scratch and Other Plays (Editor)
Falstaff (with Shakespeare, John Dennis, & William Kendrick)
Fathers and Sons
Herculaneum & Sardanapalus: Two Opera Libretti (Editor)
The Idiot
Isle of Slaves and Other Plays (Editor)
Jurgen
Justine
The Key to the Great Gate and Other Plays
The Londoners & The Green Carnation: Two Plays
Lord Jim
Mademoiselle Fifi and Other Plays (Editor)
The Madwoman of Beresina & Other Napoleonic Plays (Editor)
Mimi Pinson and Other Plays (Editor)
Notes from the Underground
Oblomov
Old Creole Days
Outrageous Women: Lady Macbeth and Other Plays (Editor)
Peter and Alexis
The Princess Casamassima
A Raw Youth
Salammbô & Dido: Two Operas (Editor)
The Stendhal Hamlet Scenarios and Other Shakespearean Shorts from the French (Editor)
Two Voltairean Plays: The Triumvirate; Comedy at Ferney
Whitewashing Julia and Other Plays
The Widow's Husband; and, Porthos in Search of an Outfit: Two Dumasian Comedies (Editor)
A Yiddish Hamlet and Other Plays
Zeneida & The Follies of Love & The Cat Who Changed into a Woman: Two Plays (Editor)

MADEMOISELLE FIFI AND OTHER PLAYS

FROM GUY DE MAUPASSANT
AND ÉMILE ZOLA

FRANK J. MORLOCK,

EDITOR

THE BORGO PRESS
MMXIII

MADEMOISELLE FIFI AND OTHER PLAYS

Copyright © 2002, 2003, 2007, 2013 by Frank J. Morlock

FIRST EDITION

Published by Wildside Press LLC

www.wildsidebooks.com

DEDICATION

For My Friend, Bill Pearlman

CONTENTS

MADEMOISELLE FIFI, by Oscar Méténier,
  Adapted from Guy de Maupassant 9
  CAST OF CHARACTERS. 11
  THE PLAY 13

MEETING, by Lucien Mayrargue, Adapted from
  Guy de Maupassant 57
  CAST OF CHARACTERS. 59
  THE PLAY 61

JACQUES DAMOUR, by Émile Zola and Léon
  Hennique 93
  CAST OF CHARACTERS. 95
  THE PLAY 97

LAZARUS, by Émile Zola. 133
  CAST OF CHARACTERS. 135
  THE PLAY 137

ABOUT THE EDITOR 151

MADEMOISELLE FIFI
BY OSCAR MÉTÉNIER, ADAPTED FROM THE NOVEL BY GUY DE MAUPASSANT

CAST OF CHARACTERS

CURÉ CHANTOVOINE

SUB-LIEUTENANT WILHELM D'EYRIK
 (Mademoiselle Fifi)

MAJOR VON FALSBERG

CAPTAIN VON KELWEINGSTEIN

LIEUTENANT OTTO VON GROSSLING

LIEUTENANT FRITZ SCHENAUBOURG

SACRISTAN

DUTY OFFICER

RACHEL

EVA THE TOMATO

BLONDINE

PAMELA

AMANDA

TWO SOLDIERS

THE PLAY

The action takes place in 1871 in the Château d'Ulville, near Rouen.

The great hall of the Château d'Ulville on the street level. In the back a large bay window opening on the park and the horizon. Some houses of the town dominated by the church clock tower rise up like an amphitheatre on the flank of a hill. Doors right and left. Near the audience to the left, a chimney, in which a large fire is burning. Near the chimney, a circular table bearing a coffee service and bottles of liquors; above it, hanging by the mirror, a rack of porcelain smoking pipes. On the walls, Flemish tapestries slashed by saber blows, and, hanging edgewise, crystal mirrors, old star-shaped cartridges, and four large family portraits in disordered piles. A warrior dressed in armor, a cardinal, a president with obscene designs around his mouth, long porcelain pipes, and a lady in costume of the Louis XV period, to which has been added, in charcoal, an enormous mustache. Arm chairs, and chairs torn up.

The Major is seated at the table and signs different

papers presented to him by the Captain, while the two lieutenants remain standing in a military posture. The Major is in undress and the lieutenants are under arms.

MAJOR

That's all?

CAPTAIN

That's all, Commandant!

MAJOR

Very good. (gaily) You will willingly take a cup of coffee, gentlemen? (rings and an orderly appears) Coffee!

(The orderly leaves, then the Captain moves his arm chair toward the chimney, places his long porcelain pipe on the circular table, and stirs the fire.)

FRITZ (low to Captain)

Go on, will you! Speak to him.

CAPTAIN (a finger on his lips)

Easy! Let's not do it abruptly! Without that we will get nowhere.

(The two lieutenants sit down and light their pipes,

which they remove from the rack and begin to smoke gravely. A silence. Outside the rain can be heard whipping the square. The Captain strolls for a minute into the hall, while the orderly returns with a platter, pours the coffee in cups, then he stops before the bay window and drums nervously on the window. A Rhenish waltz. Finally he turns.)

CAPTAIN

It's always raining!

OTTO

Since yesterday it's the same thing. A real deluge!

CAPTAIN

Since yesterday; you are being modest! For the last three months that we've been exiled to the bottom of this abominable trench known as Ulville, we haven't stopped splashing in the mud up to our ass!

MAJOR (gaily)

What's astonishing about that, gentleman, in a place geographers have disrespectfully named the chamber pot of France?

CAPTAIN

Never mind! We had no luck to be assigned to camp

in a lost country where it is not possible to procure a single distraction.— If they'd just left us at Rouen.

MAJOR

Eh! Gentlemen—war isn't waged to be amusing! My opinion is we ought to judge ourselves very lucky to have been detailed to occupy Ulville. For my part, I am enchanted to enjoy a well-earned rest here after a rough enough campaign. We are living freely, independent, peacefully in the midst of a peaceful populace, cut off from the strict discipline of general quarters. What more do you want? As for me, I have only one wish—that's to remain here until the day on which peace is definitely concluded, and we will be permitted to return to Germany.

CAPTAIN

Commandant, you are speaking as a good father of a family, a married man, well-disciplined, coming back from the vanities of this world, aspiring only to the joys of the hearth.

MAJOR

While you are a bachelor—and a confirmed one! I know your reputation, Captain. Oh! My God! If you must have distractions, why not imitate Lieutenant Eyrik? Now there's someone who's never bored for a minute!

CAPTAIN (disdainfully)

Mademoiselle Fifi! He's not a man—he's a child! A trifle amuses him!

MAJOR

Still, it's he who finds a new diversion every day. If it rains as it does today, and the weather doesn't permit him to mount his horse, he paints. (pointing to the pictures) Judge his talent! He's very ingenious. It's he who invented the mine.

CAPTAIN

The mine! That never works.

MAJOR

I beg your pardon, Captain! This morning while you were presiding at the formation he created a new experience which succeeded perfectly. Isn't that true, Lieutenant Schenaubourg?

FRITZ

Admirably. He obtained an unhoped-for result.

CAPTAIN (suddenly interested)

How's that? In what way?

MAJOR

You know quite well—the other end of the castle, in the great gallery, filled with pictures and glass cases containing a bunch of antiques, statuettes, Japanese vases, porcelains from Saxony, Chinese figurines, ivories, and Venetian cups—?

CAPTAIN

He made all that jump?

MAJOR

Why, yes!

CAPTAIN

My God! How I regret not finding myself there.

OTTO

The fact is, it was charming!

CAPTAIN

How the devil does he do it, this satanic Fifi?

FRITZ

Here's how! He filled a little China tea pot with cannon powder and into the snout he introduced a long strip of inflammable material—then he placed the engine in the adjoining room.

CAPTAIN

And then?

FRITZ

Then the device exploded, and when we entered the place there was nothing to be found. Everything was in shreds.

OTTO

You know the terracotta Venus that was in the corner to the left. Reduced to dust! Nothing remains of it except the nose! It was delicious! Ah! We had a laugh!

(All break out in laughter.)

MAJOR

But you are not telling the most curious thing about the affair! Imagine that the explosion blew a big hole in the wall and do you know what we discovered? A hiding place in which the proprietor of the castle had secreted all his silver!

CAPTAIN

Superb! And now those are indeed the feats of

Mademoiselle Fifi. But still, these are but the amusements of a little girl! It's comical—and unfortunately lasts only for a minute! Afterwards, it's necessary to seek some other thing, and it always starts all over again!

MAJOR

Ah, my word, captain, you are too difficult. And I ask myself what it would take to satisfy you.

CAPTAIN

Ah! what would it take?— Tell me, commandant, doesn't this weigh on you?

MAJOR

What?

CAPTAIN

The obligatory chastity in which we've been placed for the last three months?

MAJOR

What debauch are you planning, captain?

CAPTAIN

Well, as for me, I admit that it weighs on me, and

harshly! Eh! What the devil! To be a soldier, one is nonetheless a man! Ah, commandant, if you would permit us to organize a little party!

MAJOR

What party, captain?

CAPTAIN

I'll answer for everything, commandant! I will send the Duty Officer to Rouen, who will bring us ladies. I know where to find them—they'll prepare a supper here— Nothing besides will be lacking, at least, we will spend a pleasant evening.

MAJOR

You are mad, my friend!

FRITZ

Allow the captain to do it, commandant! It's so sad here!

MAJOR

(after a moment's hesitation) Finally! So be it! I allow it!

CAPTAIN

Ah! Bravo! Thanks, commandant!

MAJOR

Then—when will this little orgy take place?

CAPTAIN

(triumphantly) Tonight, commandant!

MAJOR

What do you mean, tonight? You will never have the time, captain—Rouen is far from here.

CAPTAIN

I had foreseen, commandant, that you would grant us the authorization necessary, and my measures have been taken.

MAJOR

Ah! Captain, you are going to make me regret—

CAPTAIN

You cannot go back on your word, commandant! A soldier's word is sacred! This morning after roll call I gave the order to the Duty Officer to hitch up a carriage, which I had covered over because of the rain, with a with a long tarpaulin, and I entrusted him with a letter to Captain Schwartz—a gallant fellow who knows some pretty girls. This evening, we will have the best of Rouen—at our service—I instructed the Duty Officer to return at six o'clock. It will soon be five—so there's a hour to wait. As for the dinner which is being prepared, you will tell me news of it, commandant!

MAJOR

Go on, I pardon you for this time, captain, but for the future, begin by warning me—without which, I will refuse. Gentlemen, I am counting that you will not make me repent of acquiescing in your desires. Remember that you are officers, and that, as such, indeed, in an enemy country, you must not depart from the courtesy one owes to ladies—regardless of the condition to which they belong.

CAPTAIN

Have no fear, commandant! (the two lieutenants bow) We know the laws of chivalry!

(The noise of a violent altercation can be heard outside.)

MAJOR

What's that again?

OTTO

Mademoiselle Fifi, who's up to his tricks again, I bet!

(The bay door opens abruptly and Sub-Lieutenant Wilhelm d'Eyrik appears, booted and spurred, a tie in his hand, brutally pushing before him a man supported by two soldiers.)

WILHELM

Commandant, I am bringing to you this lout who has permitted himself to insult me.

SACRISTAN (protesting)

Oh! Major—

WILHELM (the tie aloft)

Fie! Fie! Shut up! I was passing through the big square of the town when I met this rustic—in front of the church—to which he had the keys. It is the time that in the country they are accustomed to sounding the Angelus. I intimated to him the order to sound it—

SACRISTAN

Major, sir!

WILHELM (threatening)

Fie, I tell you!

MAJOR

Get to the point, what did he respond to you?

WILHELM

He had the audacity to refuse to do it. So I had him taken by the collar and led before you.

SACRISTAN

But not without having me mistreated—Major!

WILHELM

Not as much as you deserved, lout!

MAJOR (very calm)

Let it go, let it go, Lieutenant! (to sacristan) Why did you refuse to obey?

SACRISTAN

Major, I am only a poor man paid to do the service of the church. I've received a formal order from the curé not to ring for any ceremony. I have a family, Major, I have only my salary and my position to keep my children alive.

MAJOR

But still, as to the motive of the curé of Ulville in forbidding the ringing of the clock?

SACRISTAN (embarrassed)

I don't know—Major!

WILHELM

He must be obliged to do it, commandant!

MAJOR

Fine! Fine! Lieutenant. I will see the curé of Ulville.

(The Curé enters at the back of the stage.)

CURÉ

Major, I've just learned that my sacristan has been arrested at the door of the church, that he was beaten for no reason, dragged here between two soldiers—I demand justice of you.

MAJOR

You are arriving apropos, Mr. Curé, your sacristan pretends to have received from you a formal prohibition against sounding the clock.

CURÉ

This man is speaking the truth, Major! And that is why I demand that you set him at liberty immediately.

MAJOR

Sir, I am happy that an opportunity permits me to demand an explanation from you— For the last three months that I've been entrusted by my superiors with guarding this region, I have never abused the rights that victory gives and I have, on the contrary, given proof, as you know better than anyone, in my dealings with the local authorities of being moderate to a degree that could be haled to the most strict account. I intend, Mr. Curé, and take careful note of it, that nothing be changed in the morals and customs of the country, and since I really don't wish to bring any impediment to the acts of public life, I insist that this life resume its normal course. (to soldiers) Release that man! (to Curé) And tomorrow that the clock shall be heard at its accustomed time.

CURÉ

Major, I thank you for the generous thought which places you on the side of the innocent—but the clock of my church will not sound anymore tomorrow than today or yesterday.

MAJOR

What does this resistance to my orders signify? Take care, sir!

CURÉ

Major, when at the head of your squadron, you first set foot on the territory of this parish, you found yourself face to face with a population calm and resigned, bowing its head under the yoke of the conqueror without saying a word; but perhaps you did not feel the secret despair that this apparent resignation hides, that desires for vengeance cover the depths of these injured souls. This moderation, on which you pride yourself, was dictated by the submission that you encountered, submission that, in the ignorance you were in of the events preceding your coming, you have perhaps taken for cowardice!

WILHELM (ironic)

Indeed!

CURÉ

Listen to me in that case! I swear to you, that in my breast, as in those of all the inhabitants of this hamlet, beat patriotic hearts! One moment, it is not a question of repressing force with force— Convinced in advance of the sterility of an effort, as vain as heroic, I have choked back these awakenings of resistance, and it is thus that I have been happy to spare this flock that God has confided to my care and solicitude, from the horror of terrible reprisals. Major, it's to me that you owe it for having entered into a pacific country without any resistance.

WILHELM (in a sneering tone)

Praiseworthy prudence, and your flock must know your taste!

CURÉ (severely)

Excuse me, sir! This priestly robe, which from its color seems to wear mourning for the agony of its country, you would have found at Belfort, or at Strasbourg in the front ranks of the defenders of those noble citadels. (a silence) But here, in this humble village, without bastions or ramparts, my role changes. I am condemned to be only a man of softness—not of blood! And there remains to me only one manner of protesting against the invasion, in the name of this population whose pastor I am—this peaceful protest—the last refuge of our honor—the protest of silence! That's why Major, for the last three months, the sound of the clock has not echoed; that's why it won't resound so long as a foreign foot soils the soil of this parish!

MAJOR

I don't understand very well—

CURÉ

Then I will explain! (pointing to the clock tower on the horizon) The obstinate silence of this church, is for the rest of us, conquered without having had the opportunity to fight, the proclamation of public mourning! If the clock is an instrument of prayer, its airy voice is also a song of frivolity, and it must only sound to celebrate a happy event! Since we are not allowed to put it in motion to hurl at the flights of birds on all corners of the horizon to announce a French victory, it will remain mute!

MAJOR

Still, I could force you—

CURÉ

No, Major! The Church is the house of God, a sacred asylum, whose Lord has confided it to my care, and whose entry I forbid! The day that you wish to violate it, you will find the whole village grouped around its pastor at the foot of the altar—

WILHELM

Do you think that the whole village can prevent you

from being executed by firing squad?

CURÉ

Execute me! I am ready! You will sound the clock after that! That will be another song of victory—since it will announce the entry of a new martyr to glory—who died for his country!

(A huge silence.)

MAJOR

That's fine, Curé. You are a brave man—we are soldiers and we salute bravery. Keep the keys of your church. And do as you intend—in the future your patriotic scruples will be respected.

CURÉ

Thanks, Major; I did not expect less from your honesty and your justice!

(He bows and leaves with the sacristan.)

CAPTAIN

Well! On my oath, that Curé is a man and you did the right thing, commandant, by showing yourself generous.

MAJOR

If all the French were like him we would have had lots of trouble!

WILHELM (sullen)

Never mind, commandant, I'm mad at you for having put me in the wrong. Ah! To endure this Paternoster merchant you are losing your head. Fi! Fi! (he pronounces it "Fee, fee")

MAJOR (smiling)

Eh! Who told you, lieutenant, that I did not act purely from pure political motives— Even though I am a soldier, I am a peaceful and prudent man, and I have a horror of useless complications—

WILHELM

It would have been so amusing to make him ring-a-ding-ding his clock— Oh, just once, one single time— just for a laugh—you get so bored here!

MAJOR

Go on! gG on! Mademoiselle Fifi! This is childishness! And if it's distractions you want, the captain is here to procure them for you.

WILHELM

The Captain? What distractions?

FRITZ

It's true—you weren't here! The Captain has asked the Commandant for permission to bring women from Rouen here, and tonight there will be a big party at the castle.

WILHELM (jumping with joy)

Women! It's true, commandant? Women! Then, we are going to laugh?

CAPTAIN

Indeed, I hope so.

WILHELM

And when will they be here?

CAPTAIN (consulting his watch)

They are on the point of arriving. (night falls) But day is falling— You will excuse me? (calling) Natzi! (an orderly appears) Some lights! And a big fire! These ladies are going to arrive frozen!

FRITZ (going to the bay window)

The fact is these ladies will not have decidedly fine weather for their stroll.

OTTO

Still, it seems the shower is less violent.

(The orderly reappears, places a candelabra with several branches on the chimney, and throws an armful of wood on the fire.)

CAPTAIN

Commandant, you will allow me to perform the functions of a maître d'hôtel?

MAJOR

Do, do, Captain! You will acquit yourself very well!

CAPTAIN

We said we will be ten table companions. Rid me of all that and bring the table.

(The orderly takes out the round table and then with the assistance of another soldier brings in a long table all set and bearing rich vessels and dishes of fruits. It is lit by two candelabras.)

WILHELM (lighting a cigarette)

And the dinner, Captain? Will it be good, at least, the dinner?

CAPTAIN

You will be licking your fingers.

WILHELM

With champagne, I hope?

CAPTAIN

Champagne—in floods!

WILHELM

And where the devil were you able to procure it in this nation of pirates?

CAPTAIN

Why, the proprietor hereabouts thought of everything. And he left us a wine cellar marvelously equipped.

WILHELM

Hurrah! Hurrah! Ah! How we are going to amuse ourselves. (stopping before the portrait of the wife of Louis XV) Hold on! As for you, you will never see all this.

(Wilhelm steps back a few paces, pulls a pistol from his pocket and successively, with two shots, puts out the eyes of the portrait.)

OTTO

Well aimed, Fifi!

MAJOR

Lieutenant, it's inconceivable, the need to ravage wherever you have worked.

WILHELM

Why, it's really necessary to laugh a little, commandant!

(The noise of a carriage arriving is heard.)

FRITZ

There's the carriage! And the Duty Officer is getting out!

(They open the bay window through which all the officers rush out, and five women are led in by the Duty Officer.)

MAJOR

Ladies, be welcome!

CAPTAIN

Your clothes must be drenched!

PAMELA

No, only our cloaks are wet.

CAPTAIN

Ladies, come closer to the fire! (on a sign from the Captain the orderlies relieve the women of their cloaks and hats) Eh, why—my friend Schwartz doesn't have bad taste.

BLONDINE

You think so?

CAPTAIN

I am simply paying homage to your beauty. And I beg you to believe that I am aware of it—but the trip has given you appetite—dinner is ready; we will, if you wish it, put ourselves all at the table.

ALL

At the table!

(Otto and Fritz place their swords in a corner of the room while the Captain fusses about the women.)

CAPTAIN

Allow me! Allow me! I'm the one who arranges the order of battle! The Commandant has appointed me master of ceremonies. If you like, I am therefore going to apportion everything fairly, according to rank, so as not to disturb the hierarchy. You approve, commandant?

MAJOR

Entirely!

CAPTAIN (to the ladies)

Then come this way! (he leads them forward then dresses them in order of height: Pamela, Blondine, Amanda, Eva, and Rachel) This way we will avoid all discussion, all bickering, and all suspicion of partiality. (to Pamela) Your name?

PAMELA

Pamela!

CAPTAIN

Number one, named Pamela, adjudged to the Commandant. (to Blondine) And you?

BLONDINE

Blondine!

CAPTAIN

I get little Blondine! (hugs her) And you?

AMANDA

Amanda.

CAPTAIN

Amanda goes to Lieutenant Fritz Schenaubourg! (to Eva) And you?

EVA THE TOMATO

Eva the Tomato.

CAPTAIN

Eva the Tomato to Lieutenant Otto von Grossling. (to Rachel) And the last?

RACHEL

Rachel!

CAPTAIN

Rachel to Lieutenant Wilhelm d'Eyrik (pulling Rachel), and I have a presentiment that Mademoiselle Fifi won't be bored.

(Each officer offers an arm to the one who is designated as his, and embraces her. Wilhelm pulls Rachel forward. He takes her head as if to kiss her, and sarcastically, he blows a whiff of tobacco into her mouth. Then he starts to laugh.)

RACHEL (choking and coughing)

Say! You are not a polite little boy! Don't let it happen again—I don't like jokes of that sort.

CAPTAIN

Hey! She's not easy, Miss Rachel! Then pay no attention. He's a child! He adores to be annoying! (to Wilhelm) Mademoiselle Fifi, try to act your age, without that! Come on gentlemen, arms to the ladies and let's be seated! Pay attention, each chevalier between two ladies as much as possible! Anyway—the places are marked.

(Captain-Blondine, Major-Pamela, Fritz-Amanda,

Otto-Eva, and Wilhelm-Rachel)

OTTO (before sitting down)

We might, before beginning, escort these ladies to their rooms, where they will find brushes and soap, for after such a trip—

CAPTAIN

Not at all! Not at all! These ladies are very well as they are.

EVA THE TOMATO

(with dignity) We are clean!

CAPTAIN

I know that— You will end by not coming down— Afterwards you will want to change and that will trouble everybody.

MAJOR

The captain is right.

CAPTAIN

Always right! I am an old hand! You may serve, Natzi!

(Natzi and two other orderlies, impassive behind their

officers, begin to serve.)

MAJOR (unfolding his napkin)

Captain, you had a charming notion.

CAPTAIN

I was sure that you would thank me, commandant.

MAJOR

I am much more happy in the success of your plan since I was afraid at first that it was impracticable—

CAPTAIN

Why's that?

MAJOR

These ladies, obedient to certain scruples, might have refused.

BLONDINE

Refuse to come? Why? Because you are Prussians? (shrugging her shoulders) What can that be to us? Prussians are men like the rest—provided they pay—

AMANDA

Men in helmets must fork over!

PAMELA

Oh! First of all. It's the profession that insists upon it.

EVA THE TOMATO

And we do not have the right to be difficult, not even to choose our clients!

AMANDA

Don't we have to eat every day?

CAPTAIN (gaily)

Then eat, ladies—that's all we are asking of you—for the moment! (laughter)

PAMELA

For all that, it didn't prevent madame for not wanting to let us leave.

MAJOR

Why's that?

BLONDINE

It's forbidden by the rules. We only have the right to leave once a month—to get some rest.

EVA THE TOMATO

And she agreed to it only to please Captain Schwartz, who is an excellent client.

CAPTAIN

Oh! I recognize him plainly in that, that satanic Schwartz! I really knew what I was doing by addressing myself to him!

RACHEL (roughly pushing Wilhelm away)

And then, enough of that, you know—you!

MAJOR

What's the matter?

RACHEL

If he keeps it up, I am going to screw off. I didn't come here to be annoyed.

CAPTAIN

Look, explain yourself?

WILHELM

Fi! Fi! Naughty girl! Can't we have some fun?

RACHEL

You call that fun, do you? You've been stepping on my feet all this time, and you are jostling me—and now you just pinched me with all your might—I must have a terrible bruise.

(Exclamations by the women.)

AMANDA

Ah! Now really! That's not funny, for goodness sake!

EVA LA TOMATO

They didn't invite ladies—in that case!

BLONDINE

For sure!

RACHEL

I warn you: if it continues this is going to turn out badly.

WILHELM (sarcastically)

I would really like to see that—

RACHEL

It won't be long. You know, as for me, I have no fear.

FRITZ

Look, Wilhelm, be a little gallant—do like us.

(Fritz kisses his girl full on the mouth, and the other officers imitate him—general laughter.)

CAPTAIN

Mademoiselle Fifi, I am warning you; if you are not good I am going to send you to dine alone in your room. You will be calm? That's good, pour the champagne.

(Captain makes a sign. The orderlies pop the corks of several bottles. All drink.)

EVA THE TOMATO (like a connoisseur)

Ah! It is good!

PAMELA

There's nothing like it in the house!

RACHEL

And they make the clients pay most dearly for that, you know—

AMANDA

There's nothing to be said! It's stunning! Is nothing lacking here?

RACHEL (raging)

For what this costs them!

WILHELM

Eh! Eh! You see the insolent little thing! Well!—it's all the same to me—for I love these things. (Wilhelm seizes her and sits her on his knees; but instead of kissing her, he gnaws her cheek; blood appears and spreads down the woman's corsage, she lets out a scream. All rise. Shouts of indignation from the women.)

RACHEL (with a contained rage)

This time it's over!

MAJOR

Lieutenant, I don't understand you—you are needlessly disturbing this charming party.

(They bring some water for Rachel; she wets her napkin and stanches the blood then looks fixedly with a stony expression at Lieutenant Wilhelm.)

RACHEL

You know, that's got to be paid for!

WILHELM

I will pay.

(They all sit back down.)

CAPTAIN (slightly drunk)

Ladies, gentlemen, the incident is closed—there—since he will pay! So now, let's all be for pleasure, and since the wine's been poured, it must be drunk! (he sings) Long live wine, love, and tobacco. That's it, that's it, that's it! That's the refrain of the bivouac! And let's kiss our beauties without gnawing on them!

(All resume the refrain and embrace their girls, except Wilhelm who is brutally pushed away by Rachel.)

WILHELM (resuming the refrain)

Long live wine, love and tobacco—

MAJOR (interrupting Wilhelm with a gesture)

Gentlemen, I think the moment has come to thank our lovable guests for having responded to our call with urgency, and for having really been willing to come share our exile for an evening. Gentlemen, I drink to our ladies!

ALL

Bravo! Bravo! To our ladies!

(They click their cups.)

CAPTAIN (emphatically)

To our victories over their hearts! (new applause, bursts of laughter, general kissing) And let each pronounce his toast! You first, Otto!

OTTO (rising heroically, his cup in his hand)

To our victories over France!

(A great silence. The women, swiftly offended, rest their cups without saying a word.)

RACHEL (to Otto)

You know, I know some Frenchmen before whom you won't say that!

WILHELM

Ah! Ah! Ah! I've never seen them myself. As soon as we appear, they screw off!

RACHEL (exasperated)

You lie, swine!

(The two of them look at each other fixedly, as if they were provoking each other, eye to eye.)

WILHELM

Ah! Yes, tell us about it, beautiful! Would we be here if they were brave? (rising) We are their masters, France belongs to us! France and the French belong to us, the woods, the fields, and the houses of France!

THE OFFICERS (rising electrified, while the women remain seated silent, in consternation)

Hoch! Hoch! Dreimal hoch! Long live The Fatherland!

(They empty their cups in a single gulp.)

WILHELM (refilling his cup and placing it on Rachel's head)

The women of France belong to us, too!

RACHEL (rising with a furious gesture and causing the cup to fall and break)

Indeed! Indeed! That's not true, for goodness sake! You won't have the women of France!

WILHELM

She is so nice, this one, she is so nice! Then what did you come to do here, little one?

RACHEL

Me! Me! I am not a woman! I am a whore! Indeed, that's all the Prussians need!

(Wilhelm gives Rachel a backhanded slap; the woman seizes a knife from the table and plunges it into the officer's throat, who falls, giving a death rattle. Then she overturns a candelabra and runs out the bay window and disappears into the obscurity of the park while the other terrified women don't know where to hide. General uproar. The Captain rushes to Wilhelm and seeks to revive him.)

MAJOR (shouting)

Duty Officer! Duty Officer! Help! (stopping Otto and Fritz who are rushing towards the women) Let it go, gentlemen! Let it go! Justice will be done!

DUTY OFFICER (rushing in and saluting)

At your orders, Commandant!

MAJOR

Let the castle be searched! Let the park be closed off! Let them bring me dead or alive the woman who just left here and who just assassinated the lieutenant! And fire on whoever flees! Go! (The Duty Officer leaves. To the orderlies, pointing to the door at the left) Let these women be locked in there under careful guard! (The orderlies push the women into the room at the left; they lock the door. Turning towards the Captain) And the lieutenant?

CAPTAIN

Dead! Poor Fifi.

(They raise the body of Lieutenant Wilhelm and stretch it out all bloody on the table amidst the cups and broken bottles.)

MAJOR (roughly)

This is your fault, too, Captain! If you had not had the stupid idea of bringing this fury from Rouen here!

CAPTAIN

Could I have foreseen, Commandant?

MAJOR

One doesn't make war to amuse oneself, sir, nor to caress public women!

(Shots can be heard at unequal intervals in the park. The bay is wide open. The officers go out and attempt to see despite the darkness. They can be seen through the glass. The room is empty. The Curé enters rapidly by the door at the right; at the sight of the cadaver extended on the table he stops and removes his hat, making a sign of the cross, and begins a prayer in a low voice. Suddenly the bell tolls in the silence and continues to do so until the end of the play.)

CURÉ

The clock! They are ringing the church bell! (noticing the sacristan, who enters from the right) What's it mean?

SACRISTAN

Sir, it means that I just met the poor girl who killed this blackguard, and that they were pursuing with rifle fire. I hid her in the bell tower to turn away suspicion. I told her to toll the bell! They won't ever think of going to search up there.

CURÉ

That's good! You did well!

SACRISTAN

I was very sure that the Curé would approve. (aside) And as for me, it gives me pleasure to play a trick on these Prussian swine who so willingly massacred me this morning!

MAJOR (returning followed by officers, noticing the Curé)

You are here, sir! You let it ring, now! Is it a provocation? I warn you that I am in no mood to joke!

CURÉ

Major, death has the privilege of appeasing rancor. I am granting that by making it ring. (pointing to the cadaver) The last wish of a dying man!

(A great silence.)

MAJOR (to the Duty Officer who enters)

Well?

DUTY OFFICER

Commandant, we've search the castle high and low—we've searched in every recess of the park—we've found nothing.

MAJOR

We will be luckier tomorrow morning, no question! Set up a cordon of sentinels around the park and shoot anything that attempts to leave. Go!

(The Duty Officer salutes and leaves. The Curé kneels, as does the Sacristan, and while all the officers remove their hats and remain motionless in a respectful attitude, he begins the prayers for the dead, as the bell continues to toll.)

CURÉ

De profundis clamavi ad te, Domine, Domine exaudi vocam meam.

SACRISTAN

Fiant aures tuae intendentes, in vocem deprecationis meae—

CURTAIN

MEETING
BY LUCIEN MAYRARGUE, ADAPTED FROM A WORK BY GUY DE MAUPASSANT

CAST OF CHARACTERS

The Woman

Yves

The Man

THE PLAY

The action takes place in a sparsely furnished room. At the back, a bed with curtains.

Ordinary furniture. A door at the back. On a table near a window burns a candle. Yves, in shirtsleeves is dressing at the table, while the woman is making the bed.

WOMAN

You'll come back to see me, my dear? Tell me.

YVES

Yes, but not soon. I'm going back to the country.

WOMAN (turning to him)

Ah, you're not from here.

YVES

No.

WOMAN (curious)

Then where are you from?

YVES

From a long way away. From the Côte d'Audierne.

WOMAN

From the Côte d'Audierne. (pensively) Near Douarnez, then?

YVES

Yes, quite close. Right between 'em.

WOMAN

And it's been a long time since you went back?

YVES

Almost ten years.

WOMAN (bitterly)

Ten years. That's a long time.

YVES

Ah, yes. So I'm eager to go back.

WOMAN

And why did you stay away so long? You weren't always at sea?

YVES (somberly)

No, but I was down there. (with a large gesture) Very far away. So you see, one forgets a bit when it's a question of earning money.

WOMAN (interested)

Ah, you earned a lot?

YVES

A lot, no. You don't get rich in my profession. But still, I'm bringing back enough so the old lady can die peacefully.

WOMAN

The old lady?

YVES

Eh, by Jove, yes, My Ma! She's waiting for me. Poor ancestor.

WOMAN

And she's going to be satisfied?

YVES

For sure, to receive her son—after ten long years.

WOMAN

She's your only relative?

YVES

Yes, Pa was devoured by the Great when I was still a little kid.

WOMAN

It's sad to remain alone!

YVES

For sure! Poor Ma with two brats on her hands.

WOMAN

You have a brother?

YVES

No, a sister.

WOMAN

Still a kid?

YVES

No. By now she must be at least twenty years old, the hussy.

(tapping himself on the chest) And if she resembles her brother—

WOMAN (smiling)

She must be a pretty girl.

YVES (cheerfully)

For sure! Am I going to be happy all the same to see all that again?

WOMAN

That's going to be a rough surprise, huh?

YVES (sitting down)

Oh, yes indeed! They're going to make a face seeing me. Those who thought I'd never come back.

WOMAN

That's nice, huh, to go back there?

YVES

Yes, especially when one has, as I do (showing her his money) the wherewithal to make the folks happy.

WOMAN (interested again)

There's a lot there, a lot.

YVES (proudly)

Nearly 4,000, amassed sou by sou.

WOMAN

Four thousand francs; now that's a fortune.

(dreamily) As for me, I'll never have as much as that.

YVES

Why not, your job pays well.

WOMAN (darkly)

Ah, yoicks! You starve from January to December 31st.

YVES (also dark)

No.

WOMAN

Yes, I tell you. You're never sure you're going to get some spoiled cheese to eat the next day.

YVES (curious)

Cheese?

WOMAN (roughly)

Yeah, right. With bread, y'know.

YVES

Sorry, I didn't understand. But after ten years of living amongst savages, it's forgivable, isn't it?

WOMAN

Sure.

YVES

Anyway, where are you from?

WOMAN

From down there.

YVES

Where's that?

WOMAN (shrugging her shoulders)

What's it to you?

YVES

It's nothing to me. It was just something to talk about.

WOMAN (darkly)

I'm a Breton, too.

YVES

Ah.

WOMAN

Yes, by way of Quimper.

YVES

That's country.

WOMAN

Almost.

YVES

And why are you at Rochefort?

WOMAN

When Ma died, I followed a man.

YVES (foolishly)

You were married?

WMAN

No. He took me out of the country; he brought me here. After a couple of months he left me here with nothing.

YVES

Then?

WOMAN

So I got a job in the home of a middle-class family. After a couple weeks I was sleeping with the boss.

YVES (laughing)

That went well!

WOMAN (taking him by the arm, abruptly)

It didn't work, you see! It's really terrible, because one

fine day the Boss, having got you pregnant, boots you out.

YVES (bitterly)

You're better there than home with us.

WOMAN

Ah, you see, if these old geezers screw you, they hold on to you tight. They've got money in their pocket, they're the masters, right? Poor unlucky beggar! Ah, yes if one of 'em bleeds, the whole race can croak for all I care. If I could, I'd have done it a long while ago.

YVES

You don't like 'em?

WOMAN

I detest them! They are the ones who make us what we are: sluts! Screwing us keeps 'em young. I'd kill them all.

YVES (laughing, but a tad serious)

You're an anarchist?

WOMAN

I've got nobody.

YVES (in a kindly way)

No Pa, no Ma, no nothing?

WOMAN (hesitating)

Yes, no nothing.

YVES

Poor girl. (deciding to change the subject) And then, the Boss: where you were placed?

WOMAN

When I got fat, his wife made a scene and told me to go make babies elsewhere.

YVES

And the kid?

WOMAN (simply and sadly)

I fell in with a young guy who took pity on me. He helped me get rid of it.

YVES

Ah!

WOMAN (still sad)

So the poor little thing didn't have the trouble of coming here to suffer.

YVES (seriously)

That's a crime.

WOMAN

A crime, a crime! What is it to get a child on a poor girl who'll starve to death with it afterwards! What's a crime? It's putting a kid in the world to be cannon fodder. The poor shiver, while the rich sit by a warm fire and make kids who actually do have a Ma and a Pa. That's a crime.

(forcefully)

As for getting rid of what's in your way, not bringing something to life just to be there—that's justice.

YVES

But children have the same right to live as we do.

WOMAN

They didn't ask to come, right? What's the point of having remorse for not making those who didn't ask you to breathe and suffer?

YVES (putting on his shirt)

Poor little kids.

WOMAN (still impassioned)

Yuk! Life is a beautiful fantasy.

YVES (lightly)

If it doesn't bother you to disgust others?

WOMAN (wildly)

So you are happy!

YVES

At the moment. Because, after all these years I expect to see my Ma and little Yvonette.

WOMAN (excitedly)

Who's Yvonette, your sweetheart?

YVES

No, she's my kid sister.

WOMAN (dreamily)

Yvonette.

YVES (proudly)

Pretty name, isn't it?

WOMAN (darkly)

Yes.

YVES

And you, what's your name?

WOMAN (hesitating)

My name's Carmen. It's pretty, too?

YVES (paying no attention)

Yvonette. (dreaming) Our whole country is in that name. It's our beautiful Brittany, and the sea that I love so much, it's the sand on our beaches, it's the storm over the waves. It's all there. Yvonette!

WOMAN

You really love your Brittany, and your Ma and your Yvonette.

YVES (sincerely)

Oh, yes. (happily) And now that I've got money, I'm going to give the little one a dowry.

WOMAN

You're going to give her everything?

YVES

For sure. Two thousand for Ma, Two thousand for the little one. She won't have to marry a sailor like me. That's the way it will be when I leave again.

WOMAN

You'll leave?

YVES

Have to! To earn enough to take a rest in my turn.

WOMAN

Why not keep your money instead of giving it away?

(the storm begins; just rain and wind at first.)

YVES

The old lady worked enough when I was a kid just to keep me alive. Now it's up to me to help her.

WOMAN

So you're going back down there?

YVES

Yes. And then the old lady will have my brother-in-law around as consolation.

WOMAN

Who knows? Perhaps she's already married.

YVES

Oh, no they're waiting for me for sure. And even though they weren't sure exactly where I was, they'd have found a way to let me know. She was real cute when she was little.

WOMAN (indifferent)

All kids are cute.

YVES

No. She was really something. Huge eyes, sweet.

WOMAN

You just like her 'cause she's your sister.

YVES

But you are pretty, too.

WOMAN

Me, no! And anyway, who gives a damn! I satisfy a man. Right? That's all you can ask of me.

YVES (going close to her)

That's for sure. You're a great lover.

WOMAN (sad)

I do my best. Besides, what's the use. At any time, perhaps someone else will be here. I'm like a hotel room. You sleep in it. Next morning you leave and you forget the damned place.

YVES (kissing her)

I won't forget. You are the first girl from Brittany I've kissed in a long while.

WOMAN

Ah, bah!

YVES

That's why I didn't take the train this morning. I wanted to be completely with my family. I stopped this evening in Rochefort.

WOMAN

And you're going to leave?

YVES

Tonight. Tomorrow morning I'll be home.

(Lightning, thunder)

WOMAN

Happy?

YVES

Heck, yes. I reproach myself for leaving again right away, but I'd waited so long. I said to myself: "This is going to bring you bad luck for having passed your first pleasures." And then, my word—

WOMAN

Well?

YVES (gallantly)

It brought me luck since I met you.

WOMAN (smiling)

Thanks for the compliment.

(Lightning)

YVES

Think nothing of it.

(a clap of thunder)

Great. It's storming now.

WOMAN (going to the window)

A real squall.

YVES (going close to her)

It's true. Wind and rain. (Wind, rain lashing the window) Just like at sea. (Lightning, thunder. He makes a sign of the cross.) Holy Virgin, watch over them.

WOMAN (looking outside)

It's really coming down! A tempest.

YVES

The wind is the worst of it. (noise of wind and rain) Poor kids. Tomorrow it will surely rain. (more noise of storm)

WOMAN

Look at the street. The way people bolt and run.

YVES (looking at his watch)

And I've got to beat it, too. (lightning, thunder, wind, and rain) I've got to go now, I don't want to miss the train.

WOMAN (looking at his watch)

You've got a nice watch.

YVES (proudly)

Right. It's the only luxury I allowed myself. It's worth 160 francs.

WOMAN

That's a lot of money. (storm continues)

YVES

This is not Christian weather. If I weren't in a hurry to see my family, I'd stay the night.

WOMAN

Then stay.

YVES (looks at the bed with regret).

I can't. It's not desire or money that I lack. But really, much as I'd like to, I can't stay.

WOMAN (pouting)

Go ahead. But you are going to get soaked.

YVES

Bah! (taking his beret)

I'm a sailor. I'm used to it.

WOMAN

Don't forget me, okay? I promised to be really sweet to you and I think you were pleased.

YVES (laughing)

No, you really were sweet. So… (pulling his purse out) …I was only going to give you five, but here's fifty.

WOMAN (coldly)

Thanks.

YVES (without seeing her reaction)

Surprised you, huh? You aren't used to being spoiled.

But it's not every day I come back from a trip.

WOMAN (still cold)

Anyway, you'll come back?

YVES (kissing her)

Promise.

(Lightning, thunder, rain, and wind)

WOMAN

Don't forget. Carmen, second house coming from the arsenal. On the right.

YVES

I won't forget. (A strong gust of wind. The woman takes the candle and accompanies Yves to the door. Another gust blows out the candle. Complete night.)

YVES (outside)

Now the street light's out.

WOMAN (shouting)

Pay attention. There's a step missing.

YVES

Yes. Thanks.

WOMAN

Till soon.

YVES (far away)

See you again.

(The Woman comes back in, places the candle on the table. The stage is dark, lit only by the lightning. A Man enters from the rear)

MAN

Well?

WOMAN (turning, surprised)

Well, what? You scared me. You were there?

MAN

Likely! You've got the money?

WOMAN

What money?

MAN (brutally)

From your client, not from the Pope, for certain.

WOMAN

He gave me five francs.

(Lightning)

MAN

First of all, that's not true. He gave you ten. But I think you are satisfied with that.

WOMAN

I have to be, since he didn't owe me anymore.

MAN

What about his billfold?

WOMAN (not understanding)

What billfold?

MAN

The one he had 4000 francs in.

WOMAN

He took it with him.

MAN (furious)

Filthy slut! (lightning) You had a client with four grand and you let him leave with it.

WOMAN

I couldn't take it from him.

MAN (furious, but calming down)

No. It might be hard for you. Luckily, I was watching. (Going to the window, he opens it and looks outside)

WOMAN (terrified)

What are you going to do?

MAN

He can't have got far in this weather. (goes to door)

WOMAN (trying to bar his way)

Where are you going?

MAN (pushing her away brutally)

For a stroll.

WOMAN (trying to prevent him from leaving)

You won't go.

(He kicks her to the ground)

MAN

Screw off, okay.

(He leaves. Lightning, etc. She runs to the window)

WOMAN

Good virgin, what's he going to do?

(lightning)

The wretch who traveled so long and was so happy to be back. The other is not yet at the corner of the street.

(lightning)

He's running. He caught him. My God, they are fighting.

(lightning)

He's going to kill him. The sailor is defending himself. He's falling.

(with a raucous scream)

Murderer! Help! Help!

(the scream stops in her throat and she collapses. A moment of silence, all that can be heard is the hiccupping and weeping of the woman. Then the man returns with a bloody wound on his cheek. At least ten seconds pass. A thunderclap as the man enters.)

MAN

Good God, he was tough. He almost took my jaw off, the scum. (holding the billfold) But I've got the cash.

WOMAN (getting up)

You're back?

MAN (darkly)

Yes.

WOMAN

What did you do?

MAN

What I had to do. I wanted to take the money from him.

WOMAN (breathlessly)

And then?

MAN

He defended himself. The bugger was tough. (rubs his face)

WOMAN

Well?

MAN (cynically)

I was tougher.

(lightning)

That's all.

WOMAN

He's dead?

MAN

Dunno. Might be.

WOMAN (accusingly)

Murderer!

MAN (threateningly)

Watch what you say!

WOMAN (screaming)

Murderer! Murderer!

MAN

What manners! Argue with this. (shows her the money.)

WOMAN

Wretch!

MAN

Tweedlededee! I've got as much right to have the money as he does! (empties the billfold and puts the money in his pocket, then throws the billfold to her) How selfish I am not! I'm giving you the billfold. I'll keep the rest. And now, good evening, everybody. (he leaves. The storm continues unabated)

WOMAN

His billfold. He killed him. The poor man will never see his sister. At least his suffering is over—but her.

(lightning) His sister. Down there in the country. Poor country folks. To die, murdered like that, it's horrible.

(absently, she opens the billfold) Let's see if there are some papers in there. Heavens, his ship's book. I don't see his name. And no light in the room.

(going to the window.)

Let's wait for a flash of lightning.

(a short wait. A flash of lightning)

Yves. That's his first name.

(a pause, another flash) Lauch, from Audierne.

(lightning)

He killed my brother. Murderer! Murderer! And what am I? I sold myself to my brother, and I got him killed.

(howling)

I got my brother killed!

(Noises at the door)

What's that?

(She opens the door. Yves enters staggering)

YVES (fainting)

My Ma, My Yvonette.

(he falls)

WOMAN (falling to her knees, very gently)

My poor brother! Here I am.

(she raises his head)

I am your Yvonette.

(Yves raises himself up a little, stares at her fixedly, then falls back dead. Yvonette weeps over the body.)

CURTAIN

JACQUES DAMOUR
BY ÉMILE ZOLA AND LÉON HENNIQUE

CAST OF CHARACTERS

JACQUES DAMOUR

SAGNARD

BERRU

FELICIE

PAULINE

FRANÇOISE

THE PLAY

The action takes place at Batignolles.

A dining room, separated from a butcher shop by a glass of rough squares. In the glass partition: a small ticket window, under the window a drawer. A door not far from the ticket window by the partition to the butcher shop. A door to the right leading to the street, flanked by a window. Door to the left. A buffet, table, mahogany chairs.

Sagnard is seated at the table perusing a newspaper. Pauline and Françoise are ready to leave.

FELICIE:

Well! It's agreed, right, Françoise? You are going to take a tour of the square, not very long, and if the little girl is hungry, you will buy her a cake at the bakery.

FRANÇOISE:

Yes, Madame.

FELICIE:

(to Pauline) As for you, Pauline, I forbid you to play with the kids you don't know. You understand me?

SAGNARD:

Heavens! There are still amnestied persons returning yesterday. (perusing the paragraphs of the paper) Three hundred. They endured a storm, on departing Noumea, and their boat almost sank to the bottom.

(releasing the paper) Now, that wouldn't have been lucky, would it? Hey? Felicie, the poor devils, at the moment of seeing their native land again?

FELICIE:

Indeed.

PAULINE:

(offering her cheek to her mother) Goodbye, mama. (Felicie kisses her)

PAULINE:

(near the door) Goodbye, papa.

SAGNARD:

(who has resumed his reading) What! She doesn't kiss

her daddy before going out?

PAULINE:

Yes, indeed. This is funny. (running to him)

SAGNARD:

About time. (taking her in his arms and kissing her) There! There you go, Miss.

PAULINE:

(low to Sagnard) Give me two sous.

SAGNARD:

(low, also, laughing and ceasing to swing her around) Two sous! What for?

PAULINE:

(still low) To buy a ball.

SAGNARD:

(setting her on the ground) To buy a ball? Hum! (he pretends to hide from Felicie, fumbles in his pocket, takes out two sous, and gives them to her) My word, since your mother isn't looking—there!

PAULINE:

Thanks, papa. Are you coming, Françoise? (she leaves with Françoise)

FELICIE:

(by the door) Watch out for the traffic.

SAGNARD:

(yawning and stretching) I am going to go up and take a nap. (yawns again) Because when you've spent a night like me, the whole night at the abattoir—

FELICIE:

The fact is, you must be pretty tired, my poor man! You work too much, much too much.

SAGNARD:

Bah! a couple hours on the pillow and it won't seem that way anymore.

FELICIE:

You say that, but I repeat, you are working too much.

SAGNARD:

And as for me, if I want it, that my wife will have pretty

dresses to wear when she goes out! (Felicie shakes her head) And yes, I want our butcher shop to be the most appetizing and the most frequented in the neighborhood! Besides, doesn't the business reward us? Listen, the day when we retire from business to move to the country, won't we need a carriage? (Felicie again shakes her head) How are we going to see the child without it, when she marries in our neighborhood? Well, I'll earn our carriage. And then, you know, if one doesn't catch the eye of the young men—good night—nobody.

FELICIE:

I am happy to have known you, go! For sure, there's no better man on the earth. (tenderly) Tell me, you don't regret anything?

SAGNARD:

What's this song you are singing me?

FELICIE:

I had nothing. You just took me from my misery to be cashier-lady. Have I been all you hoped for in marrying me?

SAGNARD:

Now there are some questions! Go on, I knew quite well what I was doing, because I had judged you: I saw you so honest, heart and head firm. Today, I could leave and the shop wouldn't run badly. In the whole neighborhood, there's not a woman more understanding than you, or a man happier than me. (at a gesture from Felicie) You even doubt it a little, look—

FELICIE:

I love you, it's true! More than I loved anyone. God knows if I still wanted to try marriage!

SAGNARD:

Yes, you had bad luck with your first husband.

FELICIE:

Oh! If he hadn't been bad. I cannot say that he had been bad, even after he returned so furious, under the Commune, after having been beaten with those from Versailles. And then, he's dead, isn't he? It's already more than eight years—drowned, trying to escape down there. Heavens! Just thinking about it, I get the shivers. I know quite well he would have been able to occupy himself a bit more with me, with his child, and less with his politics, with his miserable politics. Never mind! Sometimes I think of him despite myself.

SAGNARD:

Because of the papers, I understand. They are not talking of anything else but amnesties. It's my fault, too, and I shouldn't have read the news to you just now.

FELICIE:

And what's happening with these wretches, everyday! To think he could be one of them?

SAGNARD:

You wish it?

FELICIE:

Me? No, no, surely not! I am not an ingrate; I haven't forgotten what you've done for me! And our Pauline? Poor little cat! And then, I love you. You want to make me repeat it, huh? (hugging him) My brave man, go! Oh—oh—oh! You didn't put on your tie today? Are you always going to forget, every morning, to put on your tie?

SAGNARD:

(radiant) It's you who make me lose my head. Heavens! I have no wish to sleep now.

FELICIE:

That won't prevent you from sleeping all the same. Look, an hour, just one hour to get rid of your exhaustion a little. An hour! That's not much!

SAGNARD:

You promise to come wake me up in an hour?

FELICIE:

I promise.

SAGNARD:

(after having kissed her) Then I'm going up. (stopping a moment before leaving) All the same! all those papers with their amnesties are starting to get on my nerves! I won't buy any more. (to Felicie) Till later. (he leaves)

(Felicie prowls around for a moment opening and shutting drawers. Berru enters by the door which gives on the little street. He's a bit drunk.)

BERRU:

Hello, Madame Sagnard.

FELICIE:

Berru!

BERRU:

Himself, Madame Sagnard, my beautiful Madame Sagnard. Hey! It's a long time that we haven't seen each other? Almost eight years.

FELICIE:

Berru!

BERRU:

Eh! Yes, Berru! That funny old Berru! A friend, what! The pal of your first husband, Jacques Damour! (a silence) Have I really aged, changed so much, that I astonish you like this? (silence) And me, I was coming like an old comrade, like in the days of that poor Jacques. (another silence) Then you've still got it in for me? (gesture by Felicie) Hey! What! Damour in the New World, you were, indeed, free not to have it in for me! One flirts with someone, they don't suit; no reason to quarrel. That would work, much better! That wasn't so much the worse! Didn't I have to go?

FELICIE:

(harshly) How can I help you?

BERRU:

I was passing by. Then I said to myself: let's go in to see Madame Sagnard.

FELICIE:

Well! You've seen me. Goodnight!

BERRU:

You are hard, Madame Sagnard. Can't one come ask for news of one's friends? And your daughter, Louise, what's become of her?

FELICIE:

(troubled) Louise, Louise— You didn't come for her, did you? Then what? What is it you want from me?

BERRU:

Your husband of today, Citizen Sagnard, is he here?

FELICIE:

Yes, he's asleep. You want to speak to him?

BERRU:

No, only to you. What a hurry you are in, slow down! (casting a glance at the furniture) Ah! Indeed, ah! Indeed, say there. By Jove! Sonofabitch! It is rich, your little hovel! Mahogany, like it was raining! A real dining room of a swell! It's more dashing at your place than it used to be. You remember the Rue Envierges at Menilmontant? As for me, I can still see you there. There were three rooms. Yours, where you slept with Damour, that of your brother-in-law, Eugene, of that poor Eugene. (he removes his cap) Executed by firing squad! And a dining room where they put bench vices to work—not counting the kitchen and Louise's little room. We got drunk in that lodging! You didn't have fine furniture at that period, but it was great fun all the same. Wasn't it, Madame Sagnard? (a silence) As for me, my dream would have been to see you installed as you are here, but with my old buddy Damour.

FELICIE:

Is this finished? Are you going to leave me in peace? How did you dare to present yourself in my home? You, for indeed, I know what I know, perhaps! It was you who disturbed my first household. (Berru gestures in protest) Yes, it was you who debauched Damour; it's you who put a rifle in his hands. (new protest from Berru) If he hadn't kept bad company—

BERRU:

He only kept company with me.

FELICIE:

That sufficed.

BERRU:

Keep the insults to yourself, old pal. Ah! good God, now that's how they judge you, and it will always be like that. Still, I spared him many stupidities! If he had listened to me, he would never have been sent to Noumea. Do you hear me? Never! (Felicie shrugs) As for me, I kept out of it.

FELICIE:

You never fought. You were in the commissariat.

BERRU:

What's that prove? (in a voice almost deep) They don't have rifles in the commissariat? (looking around him) That I demolished! (aloud) Only after, I was sharp.

FELICIE:

Very sharp.

BERRU:

For all that, you haven't been sharp? You didn't get yourself out of it? Once Damour disappeared, didn't you marry one of the richest of the rich, the biggest butcher in Batignolles? So what do you call that? Sacrificing yourself? Ho! Wow!

FELICIE:

I did what I wished. And that's enough of this, isn't it? I knew you, and I repeat, that it was you who led Damour, who was the best of men, astray. Oh! It's not that you were evil, but you were a weak man and a drunkard, we were sure to see you show up when we had a good bite to eat and full liters of wine. Yes, yes, you smelled the cooking from a distance.

BERRU:

There's nothing evil in that.

FELICIE:

During the siege, you were hiding at our place to eat our white bread. Well, my brave man, you are deceiving yourself, if you think that's going to start over again here. No more guzzling; do me the pleasure of taking the door.

BERRU:

Fine! Fine! We will see about all that soon! Really, you are wrong to be so proud. Do you believe, my beautiful Madame Sagnard, that if Damour returns he won't strangle you, you and the whole crew?

FELICIE:

Damour is dead.

BERRU:

A conjecture, that he isn't dead. That he may be waiting for me on the boulevard two steps from here.

FELICIE:

(interrupting him) Is that all you came here to tell me?

BERRU:

Perhaps!

(Knocking on the window of the butcher shop, Felicie goes to open it.)

A MAN'S VOICE:

Two pounds of the filet at two and a quarter.

(Berru goes to the street door, opens it and signals Damour, who enters and stands behind him.)

FELICIE:

Are things going well, Miss Marie?

A WOMAN'S VOICE:

Very well, Madame, and the child?

FELICIE:

The child is out walking. I thank you.

(Felicie returns the money, shuts the window, and, hand in her drawer, removes the money for a moment.)

FELICIE:

(turning to Berru) What! You are still here? You haven't finished boring me?

BERRU:

Me, yes. (effacing himself) But, wait! Here's a comrade who wishes to speak with you.

FELICIE:

(not recognizing Damour, who is miserably dressed with a long beard) You have something to ask of me? (a silence) What can I do for your service, sir? (stifling a scream and releasing into the drawer the fistful of money which she had kept) You! What! It's you! It's you.

(Damour keeps silent.)

BERRU:

Yes, he's been looking for you for the last two weeks. Then, he met me and I led him here. Friends are friends.

FELICIE:

(getting control of herself, bit by bit) Look, Jacques, what have you come here to ask of me? (another silence) I remarried, it's true. But, it's not my fault, you know it. I thought you were dead, and you did nothing to get me out of the error.

DAMOUR:

Yes, I wrote you.

FELICIE:

You wrote me?

DAMOUR:

That's what I'm telling you.

FELICIE:

I swear that I never received your letters. You know me, you know that I've never lied. Still, you were dead. And, hold it! I have the death certificate here in a drawer.

(Felicie goes to a desk, opens it, and extracts a paper which she gives to Damour who starts reading it with a stupid air.)

DAMOUR:

(stammering) The certificate—the certificate.

FELICIE:

So, I saw myself completely alone. I gave in to the offer

of a man who wanted to take me out of my misery and torments. That's the extent of my fault. It's not a crime, is it? And you have nothing to reproach me with. I allowed myself to be tempted by the idea of being happy.

DAMOUR:

You hadn't been before, with me?

FELICIE:

Not always Jacques— Remember.

DAMOUR:

I wrote you. As for me, that's all I see.

FELICIE:

I changed my address from the neighborhood. They hunted me everywhere. Where were you the last time you wrote me?

DAMOUR:

In America— Down there, in Noumea, I had no news of you, I was no longer living, and I escaped with three comrades who were drowned. Then, they thought they recognized me in one of them. I learned that from a newspaper.

BERRU:

A famous piece of luck you had to escape from there, my old friend!

DAMOUR:

Not so famous! (he looks at Felicie broken-hearted)

FELICIE:

What do you want? I didn't know anything.

DAMOUR:

I worked in the gold mines, to bring you back a fortune. I thought only of you. Which almost enslaved me, good breeding! One moment I had almost forty thousand francs in an old handkerchief. Then, all this went. They robbed me. Then I came back. Not daring to debark in France, I went to Belgium, I worked in the coal mines at Mons, underground, and I hardly made wherewithal to keep from croaking of hunger. You hadn't answered, me, too, I thought you were dead. One night, in a cabaret, I heard tell that an amnesty had had been voted and that all the members of the Commune could return to Paris. And I don't know what went through my head. I came down with a fever of coming back. I no longer saw you dead, I imagined Louise grown. I thought that you were waiting for me, that I was going to find you in the Rue des Envierges, that a table would be waiting with a bouquet in the middle to celebrate me. (in a strangled voice) But don't believe it! Not often! Misfortune upon misfortune! It almost killed me, dammit!

FELICIE:

My poor Jacques!

DAMOUR:

In Paris, I sought you everywhere. But what's the good of telling you all I suffered here! The employers don't want me. A Communard! It never failed! Besides, they told me that I was too old. I was going to throw myself in the water when I met Berru.

BERRU:

Ah! That was a real surprise. But you were dead! That's what I told him. You know, old boy, if I was expecting this!

DAMOUR:

(to Felicie) Finally, here I am. (a silence) Where is my daughter?

FELICIE:

Your daughter?

DAMOUR:

Yes. Where is Louise?

FELICIE:

(lowering her head) She is dead.

DAMOUR:

(with a cry of sadness) Dead— My God!

(Pauline and Françoise enter. Pauline rushes to her mother and leaps on her neck.)

PAULINE:

It's us, little mother. Françoise said it was time to come home. Oh! If you knew, there's sand, and there are ducks in the water.

FELICIE:

(uneasy) That's fine, leave me. Françoise, take her. It's stupid to return so soon.

FRANÇOISE:

But, Madame—

FELICIE:

Take her back, go!

(Pauline and Françoise leave.)

BERRU:

The little Sagnard—huh? The seed of brats grows quickly!

DAMOUR:

(banging his fist on the table) That's not all! I've come to take you back!

FELICIE:

(trembling) Sit down and let's talk. Making an uproar won't advance things. So, you are coming to find me?

DAMOUR:

Yes, you are going to follow me, and right away. Right, Berru? I am your husband, the only good one. Oh, I know my rights. Isn't that right, Berru, it's my lawful right? Come on, put on a bonnet, be sweet, if you don't want the world to know our business. (Felicie doesn't answer) You refuse? I understand. You are accustomed now to play the lady at the cashier's desk; and as for me, I don't have a beautiful shop, nor a drawer full of money that you can play with at your ease. Then, there's the little girl, just now, who you seem to me to care more for than Louise. If they've let the daughter run off, they make fun of the father! But that's all the same to me. I intend for you to come, and indeed you will come or I will go to the police and I will return with the cops. That's my right.

FELICIE:

Listen, Jacques.

DAMOUR:

It's my right— Isn't it, Berru?

BERRU:

(sententiously) Yes, it's your right; but we have to see; as for me, I am for doing things without getting into a passion. (to Felicie) Unfortunately, the lady is rushed. It's hard to wait in her position. Ah! Madame, if you knew! Not a radish, he's starving.

FELICIE:

Pardon me, Jacques. (a silence) What's done is done. But I don't want you to be unhappy. Let me come to your aid.

(Violent gesture from Damour.)

BERRU:

(excitedly) Quite, certainly. (to Damour) The house here is full enough, so that your wife won't be leaving the womb empty. (to Felicie) Why don't you give him a little something to keep the pot boiling, so he can make a little bouillon.

FELICIE:

Oh! As much as he would like, Mr. Berru.

BERRU:

(to Damour) Look, would you really accept a gift? A meal and some cutlets.

DAMOUR:

Thanks, I don't eat bread like that. (coming and looking Felicie in the eyes) It's you alone that I want, and I will have you.

FELICIE:

(recoiling) My God!

DAMOUR:

(getting carried away) Damnation! It's not enough to have suffered what I have suffered, it's still necessary for me to be scorned! Do you want me to break everything here! Let's go! Tell the truth; if Louise is dead, it's because you deserted her. (he shakes her violently) Ah! If I was sure of it.

FELICIE:

(without defending herself) Oh! Jacques! Jacques!

BERRU:

Calm down! You are going to ruin your position.

DAMOUR:

Leave me alone. (to Felicie) Do you intend to follow me, yes or no?

FELICIE:

Why I cannot—I cannot.

DAMOUR:

You cannot? (he grasps a chair and raises it) Heavens! I'm going to hurt you.

BERRU:

(disarming Damour) Hey! Nothing stupid.

DAMOUR:

I'd better go, I'm going to kill her!

BERRU:

(to Felicie) That's it, I'll take him away for a minute.

DAMOUR:

(to Felicie) Yes, I'm going away. But you won't lose anything by waiting. I will return and watch out below, you, the kid, and the whole camp. Expect me, you will see!

SAGNARD:

(entering excitedly) What's the matter then?

(Felicie, petrified, doesn't budge.)

DAMOUR:

(furious, raising his fist) What's wrong is—

BERRU:

(to Sagnard) Mrs. Sagnard will tell you about it, sir. That will be best. (dragging Damour) Let's go, come.

(Berru and Damour leave by the street door.)

SAGNARD:

What's the matter with him? Who are these two men?

FELICIE:

(stammering) It's—it's Berru.

SAGNARD:

Who's that, Berru?

(Knocking on the cashier's cage, Felicie opens.)

FELICIE:

How much to receive?

A VOICE:

Seven-fifty, Madame.

(Felicie takes the money, shuts the cage, then turns, all pale and trembling.)

SAGNARD:

Look, Felicie, what's wrong with you? Why are you trembling? Who were those two men?

FELICIE:

He's come back.

SAGNARD:

Who?

FELICIE:

My husband.

SAGNARD:

What husband?

FELICIE:

Damour.

SAGNARD:

The one who was dead?

FELICIE:

(bursting into tears) He's come back, I tell you. And he wants to take me away.

SAGNARD:

To take you away? Why, he's mad.

FELICIE:

(on Sagnard's breast) He is not mad. I told him all that one can say to a man; but he wasn't listening, he's out of his head, he's talking about massacring all of us.

SAGNARD:

(after a silence) Would you like to know what causes me the most pain in all this? It's that you are in the process of blaming yourself. He's come back, well! So what? Do you think I will let him take you away? Ah! No, for goodness sake! My God! There's nothing funny about it, I understand that very well, but it will end by working itself out all the same! Won't everything work out? I will speak to him.

FELICIE:

You want to talk to him?

SAGNARD:

Heavens! By Jove! He's not the one to frighten me! I've seen others.

FELICIE:

Now they are going to fight! My God! How miserable I am!

SAGNARD:

Perhaps he won't devour me.

FELICIE:

(still weeping, at the table, head in her hands) My God! My God!

SAGNARD:

Can one make oneself so upset like that? Yes, it's possible. Look, Felicie—

(Enter little Pauline. She stops, speechless, looks at her father, and he gestures to her to go to Felicie.)

PAULINE:

You are weeping, mama? Why are you weeping? Who has caused you pain?

FELICIE:

Nobody, my poor little cat.

PAULINE:

Then don't cry any more, mama. Don't cry any more, I tell you. Here! Give me your handkerchief, so I can dry your eyes. I am nice, huh? (drying her mother's eyes)

SAGNARD:

(standing near his wife) Is it over?

PAULINE:

First of all, mama, if you cry again, I am going to cry, too.

FELICIE:

It's over. (she hugs her)

(Enter Damour and Berru.)

FELICIE:

(noticing Damour) Lord! He's here again!

(Damour comes forward. Sagnard quickly places himself between him and Felicie, who runs off dragging Pauline. A silence during which the two men look at each other.)

SAGNARD:

Then, it's you?

DAMOUR:

Yes, it's me.

SAGNARD:

Very well. Let's talk it over.

DAMOUR:

(hesitating) It's—it's not you with whom I wish to speak, it's to Felicie.

SAGNARD:

Look, my comrade, let's have an explanation straight away. What the devil! We have nothing to reproach one another for. Why devour each other, when it's nobody's fault?

DAMOUR:

(in a heavy voice) I haven't got it in for you; leave me alone, get out of here. It's to Felicie that I wish to speak.

SAGNARD:

(calmly) As to that, no, you won't speak to her. I have no wish that you make her ill. We can discuss things without her. Besides, if you are reasonable, everything will be fine. Since you appear to love her still, look at your position, consider, and act for her good.

DAMOUR:

(excitedly) Shut up! Don't meddle with this or it's going to turn out badly. (he advances on Sagnard)

BERRU:

(interposing) Look, Damour. You promised me.

DAMOUR:

Leave me alone, okay! What are you afraid of? You're an idiot!

SAGNARD:

Calm down, comrade, calm down! Look, as for me, am I enraged? If you are enraged, you don't know what you are doing. (a silence) Listen, if I call Felicie, promise me to be good, because she is very sensitive, you know that as well as I do. Neither of us wants to kill her, right? You will behave properly?

DAMOUR

(in a dolorous and profound tone) If I'd come to behave badly, I would have begun by strangling you, you with all your talk.

SAGNARD:

Then I am going to call Felicie. Oh! As for me, I am very fair; I understand that you wish to discuss the thing with her. It's your right. (knocking on the door of her room) Felicie! Felicie! (silence) Felicie, come on. (impatiently after a new silence) What you are doing is stupid. He's promised to be reasonable.

(Felicie enters, eyes red.)

BERRU:

(aside) Here's a sudden downpour!

(Sagnard stands at the window, raises the curtain with a finger, and affects to look outside.)

DAMOUR:

Listen, Felicie, you know that I have never been bad. That you can say. Well, today's not the day I will begin to be so. First of all, it's true, I wanted to slaughter all of you here. Then, suddenly, as I left, I asked myself how that would help me. I prefer to let the mistress choose. We will do what you wish. Yes, since the courts can do nothing for us with their justice, it's you who will decide which of us pleases you better. Answer. With whom do you want to be, Felicie?

FELICIE:

(in a strangled voice) My God!

DAMOUR:

Yes, with whom? (silence by Felicie) That's fine, I understand. It's with him you want to be. Returning, I know how this upsets everything. And I don't wish you ill for it, I am fair after all. As for me, I am finished, I have nothing in the end, you no longer love me; as for him, he will make you happy, without even counting the little girl I saw. (Felicie weeps) You are wrong to cry, these are not reproaches. Things have turned out this way, that's all. And then, I want to tell you that you can sleep peacefully. Now that you have chosen, I won't bother you anymore. It's over; you won't hear any talk of me anymore. Goodbye!

(He heads toward the door. Sagnard stops him.)

SAGNARD:

Ah! You are a brave man, for goodness sake! It's not possible for you to leave this way. You are going to dine with us.

DAMOUR:

No, thanks.

BERRU:

What, you refuse?

SAGNARD:

At least we will drink a glass. You will, indeed, accept a glass of wine with us, what the devil?

DAMOUR:

(eyes on Felicie who begs him with a look) Yes, all the

same.

BERRU:

(gaily) Let's go to it!

SAGNARD:

(enchanted) Quick, Felicie, some glasses. We don't need the maid. Four glasses. You must drink also. (To Damour) Ah, comrade, you are really nice to accept, you don't know the pleasure you are doing me; because, for me, I like good hearts, and you, you are a good heart, I'll answer for that.

BERRU:

For sure he's a good heart. (poking Damour in the stomach) Hey! Laugh now, my old rabbit!

(Damour smiles sadly. Felicie pours a drink. A short silence.)

SAGNARD:

Here's to you!

(Sagnard extends his glass. Felicie extends hers.)

DAMOUR:

(clinking with Felicie) Here's to you.

(They drink in silence.)

BERRU:

Famous, that wine!

PAULINE'S VOICE:

(outside, tapping on the door) Mama! Mama!

FELICIE:

Right away.

DAMOUR:

(after having put his glass on the table) That's it! Goodbye, everybody!

(He leaves.)

CURTAIN

LAZARUS
BY ÉMILE ZOLA

CAST OF CHARACTERS

CHORUS

JESUS

MOTHER

SPOUSE

CHILD

LAZARUS

THE PLAY

A deep and savage grotto. To the left, through an opening, a ray of light falls through a narrow gorge. Some blocks of rocks have rolled into the midst of the grotto. It's against one of these rocks that Lazarus' tomb is found; a simple opening hollowed into the earthen rock, which is covered with a heavy slab.

CHORUS:

Lazarus is dead, O Jesus, and we've been weeping for him for the last four days, despairing, all of us, his friends. Here's the tomb where we laid him with our charitable hands. And we are bringing you here, you who walk on water, and who reopen to the light the dead eyes of the blind, so that you can restore him living to our affection. A word from you, all powerful master, and he will revive.

JESUS:

Lazarus is dead and my heart is filled with infinite pity. With you, I weep for him; I weep for the misery of suffering humanity. Why reawaken him to this life of terrible torments?

CHORUS:

We loved him so much, we want him among us, to love him still. Look at your feet: his mother is there, and his spouse, and his child, who beg you to return him to them.

JESUS:

When one has lived, one has done his duty; it would be unjust and cruel to revive him. My mercy, my immense goodness goes to poor creatures freed of accomplished labor, who sleep under the eternal earth a good refreshing sleep.

MOTHER:

Oh, Jesus, Lazarus is dead, and I'm his mother. My torn womb cries to you, you, who with a word can close my wound. All the blood of my veins is leaving with my poor child who is gone. Don't you know that I gave him the best of myself, of my suffering, and of my tenderness? He came out of my flesh, he drank my milk, he grew in my tears—beneath each of my wrinkles is a misfortune of his. Return him to me, even if it's necessary that he suffer and that I suffer again. As a child, I kept him on my knee to protect him, without budging, from death which was prowling about. Return him to me; we will weep together; and we will be happy.

JESUS:

Ah, poor mother, how I wish you to be happy.

SPOUSE:

I am the spouse, O Jesus, and Lazarus is dead, and I want you to return him to my caresses. In giving me our child he became me. It's as if half of myself has left, fallen into dust there in this tomb. We loved each other with all our hearts, with all our flesh. The wind can no longer pass through my hair without my remembering his kisses. I shiver everywhere in the sun recalling his embrace. And now here I am alone in my bed. I am quite lost and frozen. Return him to me so that I can warm him in my loving arms. Return him to me so I can take him again in my heart and so the world will no longer be empty.

JESUS:

Ah! Poor wife, poor lover, how I want to console you!

CHILD:

As for me, I am the child, O Jesus. Lazarus is dead, my father is dead, and I am orphan, the frail young offshoot at the foot of the great downbeaten oak. All my young being is terrified and exhausted; return to me his kindly shadow so I can grow in strength and beauty. I have only my weakness and my grace to touch you, and I hold them out to you. I am so small, so shivering, so artless that you cannot leave me there alone on the way. O good friend of little children, give me back my father.

JESUS:

Ah, poor child, dear child, whose tears I would like to dry.

CHORUS:

You hear them. They implore you and we implore you with them. Why are you resisting their tears? You loved Lazarus as much as we. Give to the world a shining example of your power and your love. Perform this miracle.

MOTHER:

Perform this miracle, return my son to me. And let all mothers adore you on their knees!

SPOUSE:

Perform this miracle, return my husband to me, and each kiss of mine will glorify you.

CHILD:

Perform this miracle, return my father to me, so that little children will bless you at night.

CHORUS:

Perform this miracle. Give to the world a shining example of your power and your love.

JESUS:

You wish it; I accede to your lamentations, insatiable creatures, thirsty dreamers of the eternal living sorrow. But my heart is full of anguish; no man has known the misfortune of returning from the dead. Ah, divine pity, delightful pity, death consoles where all beings rest! You wish it, you wish it, this terrible example?

ALL:

Yes, yes, reawaken Lazarus, and you will be God and we will bless you, we will adore you.

JESUS:

Raise the stone. (three men raise the lid which they keep standing against the rock. Lazarus appears lying in the tomb, wrapped in his shroud.) Lazarus, arise! (a silence) Lazarus, arise!

LAZARUS:

(motionless, in a weak voice) Who's calling me?

JESUS:

Lazarus, arise!

LAZARUS:

(still motionless) Is it you, O Jesus, who troubles my sleep?

JESUS:

Lazarus, arise!

LAZARUS:

(sitting up) O Jesus, I was sleeping so well.

JESUS:

Lazarus, arise!

LAZARUS:

(standing, getting out of the tomb supported by two friends) It was so good, O Jesus, this great dark sleep, this great dreamless sleep. Never had I known the sweetness of absolute repose. It's only in the tomb. Still, I slept, I was reposing in the delightful infinities of the night and of silence. Nothing came from the earth anymore, neither the echo of a noise, nor the chill of a day. And I was motionless, ah, the eternal immobility, the endless bliss, so divine in the annihilation of the world. O Master, why have you reawakened me? Why this cruelty of snatching the poor dead from his joy of tasting the eternity of sleep? It hardly began; I had thousands and thousands of years to sleep. And it was so good, it was so good.

JESUS:

Poor being, these are your friends, they are your relations, who desired it for their happiness. You are going to live again.

LAZARUS:

Live again, oh! No, oh! No! Haven't I paid with suffering my frightful debt of living? I was born without knowing why; I lived without knowing how, and you would make me pay double, you would condemn me to start my time of hardship over on this sorrowful earth. What inexplicable sin have I committed for you to punish me with such a chastisement? To live again, alas! To feel oneself die a little each day in his flesh, having the intelligence only to suspect, the will but not the power, the tenderness to weep for the sorrows of my heart. And it was over, I had leaped over death, this second so horrible that it suffices to poison your entire life. I felt the sweat of agony soak me, the blood withdrew from my members, my breath escaped in a last death rattle. And this affliction, you want me to experience it twice? That I die twice and that my human suffering exceed that of all men. Oh, no, Master, oh, no!

MOTHER:

Lazarus, don't you recognize me? I am your mother, and my bosom crackled with glee when I saw you living, standing. Ah, what prodigious joy to hear you again, to have you still. Come, let me escort you, let me take care of you as in the long distant days when you were little.

LAZARUS:

No, no, mother. Love me enough to leave me to solitary happiness. What new suffering, if living, I were to lose you! Soon you will rejoin me and you will see how good it is, how good it is. When one has known the delights of this sleep, there's no comparable joy on earth.

SPOUSE:

And as for me, Lazarus, me, your wife who sighs after your embrace and who shudders there, when your voice passed over the nape of my neck like a June breeze. Don't you want to know me anymore and make my happiness?

LAZARUS:

O wife, darling wife, I am no better than an unfaithful spouse who has slept in the bed of another, the softest, the most tempting, the most unforgettable. I have slept with death, the eternal lover, and it was so good, so good to sleep in the arms of silence and of night that my lips are no longer made for the lips of the living.

CHILD:

And as for me, father, your child, are you going to forget me? You took my small hand, you led me by the ways. Are you going to leave me thus, all alone? And you repeated to me every morning that we must love life.

LAZARUS:

Life, oh, I loved it with all my strength, with all my passion. I lived as one loves, I gave myself completely to the joy of being. And it's thus, my child, that you will live and continue my work! Your mother is there to guide you. As for me, I performed my task and I went to bed, day came, and no one has the right to awaken me from my slumber, from my good sleep.

JESUS:

You don't wish to live again? O my brother, o poor man, you make my tears flow.

LAZARUS:

No, no. Don't inflict the torment of living on me again. This torture is so frightful that you have never condemned any man to it. I've always loved you and served you, O Master, don't make me the greatest example of your wrath which will dismay generations.

CHILD:

Father, have you seen heaven? Is it for this you are leaving us?

SPOUSE:

What superhuman delights recall you to paradise?

MOTHER:

Tell us what you've seen from the other side of the wall from which no one ever returns.

LAZARUS:

Nothing, nothing, nothing. I slept: the black immensity, the infinity of silence. Why, if you knew how good it was, to no longer be, to sleep in the nothingness of all. O Master, if you can do it, I beg you perform this other great miracle so I can sleep in this tomb again without suffering, I can receive my eternal interrupted sleep. O my mother, O my wife, O my child, O my friends, if you love me, do me justice, beg Jesus to return me to the sweet death from which no one had the right to bring me back.

MOTHER:

Perform this miracle again. I love my son enough to want only his joy. Let him sleep while waiting for me, since he knows where happiness is.

SPOUSE:

I implore you, also, perform this miracle. The memory of our kisses will be more ardent than this pale ghost from the tomb. And I will be happy if he is happy.

CHILD:

My father is tired, perform this miracle so he can sleep again without suffering. Life won't cease, for I am here to continue life.

CHORUS:

Without pain, we conjure you that Lazarus shall not suffer more; he mustn't suffer more. Perform this miracle and let Lazarus resume sleep without pain.

JESUS:

Yes, yes, without pain this time, poor Lazarus. You would have it, and you've understood, you know now. After the passion of life, death is the great comforter. My austere heart bleeds for him from the effort to revive him. And it is wise, it is just, it is good, that he sleep again.

LAZARUS:

O Jesus, thanks! (he goes back into the tomb)

JESUS:

Lazarus, go back to sleep. (Lazarus lies down) Lazarus go back to sleep.

LAZARUS:

(in a weak voice) What sweetness! Thanks, O Jesus.

JESUS:

Lazarus, go back to sleep.

LAZARUS:

(lower and lower) The black immensity, the infinity of silence. O Jesus thanks. (his voice is extinguished.)

JESUS:

Lazarus, go back to sleep. (a great silence) Replace the stone. (the three men replace the slab on the tomb) Ah! Poor human creature, creature of suffering and of misery, sleep. Sleep now—forever happy and for eternity.

ALL:

Ah! Poor Lazarus, poor tired man, broken by misery and suffering, sleep, sleep now, happy forever, for eternity.

CURTAIN

ABOUT THE EDITOR

Frank J. Morlock has written and translated many plays since retiring from the legal profession in 1992. His translations have also appeared on Project Gutenberg, the Alexandre Dumas Père web page, Literature in the Age of Napoléon, Infinite Artistries.com, and Munsey's (formerly Blackmask). In 2006 he received an award from the North American Jules Verne Society for his translations of Verne's plays. He lives and works in México.

www.ingramcontent.com/pod-product-compliance
Lightning Source LLC
LaVergne TN
LVHW041627070426
835507LV00008B/483